OH, THE PLACES HE WENT

A Creative Minds Biography

OH, THE PLACES HE WENT

A Story about Dr. Seuss—
Theodor Seuss Geisel

by Maryann N. Weidt

illustrations by Kerry Maguire

M Millbrook Press/Minneapolis

To the Dooleys, especially the Flying Irishman

My thanks to Audrey Geisel, Claudia Prescott, Gordon Calderwood, Barbara Cole, Liz Cook, Mary Dryden, David Groce, Judith and Neil Morgan, Robert Sullivan, Bonnie Wallin, and Barbara and Karl ZoBell. Thanks also to Herbert Cheyette, of International Creative Management, Inc., for assistance regarding use of the Dr. Seuss characters in the illustrations.

A special thank-you to Peggy Owens, Ted's niece, who spent countless hours sharing childhood memories and helping me get the facts straight. Thank you also to my editor, Marybeth Lorbiecki, who helps me *keep* the facts straight.

Text copyright © 1994 by Maryann N. Weidt
Illustrations copyright © 1994 by Kerry Maguire

This book is available in two editions:
Library binding by Millbrook Press, a division of Lerner Publishing Group, Inc.
Soft cover by LernerClassroom, an imprint of Lerner Publishing Group, Inc.
241 First Avenue North
Minneapolis, MN 55401 USA

For reading levels and more information,
look up this title at www.lernerbooks.com.

Library of Congress Cataloging-in-Publication Data

Weidt, Maryann N.
    Oh, the places he went : a story about Dr. Seuss—Theodor Seuss Geisel / by Maryann N. Weidt ; illustrated by Kerry Maguire.
        p.   cm. — (creative minds book)
    ISBN 978–0–87614–823–5 (lib. bdg. : alk. paper)
    ISBN 978–0–87614–627–9 (pbk. : alk. paper)
    ISBN 978–0–8225–3597–3 (eBook)
    1. Seuss, Dr.—Juvenile literature. 2. Authors, American—20th century— Biography—Juvenile literature. 3. Illustrators—United States—Biography—Juvenile literature. 4. Children's literature—Authorship—Juvenile literature. [1. Seuss, Dr. 2. Authors, American. 3. Illustrators.] I. Maguire, Kerry, ill. II. Title. III. Series.
PS3513.E2Z93   1994
813'.52—dc2O   93-41370

Manufactured in the United States of America
16 – CG – 1/1/14

1

On Fairfield Street

The grandfather clock in the hall chimed twice. Theodor Seuss Geisel, who was called Ted, lay on his bed in his house on Fairfield Street, in Springfield, Massachusetts. He listened. He heard the wind blow softly through the elms and maples in the backyard. Then came the sound he had been waiting to hear—AWOOOOOOOOOOOOOOooooo.

It was the wolves. But Ted was not frightened. Many nights he had been awakened by their howling. They lived just six blocks away, at the Forest Park Zoo.

Four-year-old Ted sat up and peered out his window at the fields behind the house. One lonely farmhouse stared back. His sister Marnie, who was two years older, had said the place was haunted.

Ted didn't know if he should believe Marnie or not. She was always making up stories and words. In fact, she even invented her name. Her real name was Margaretha, but when anyone asked her, she would say, "Marnie Mecca Ding Ding Guy." Soon everyone was calling her Marnie.

In that year, 1908, the Forest Park Zoo was part of a 700-acre park. Ted's father, who was named Theodor *Robert* Geisel, was a volunteer park commissioner. In the summer, Ted and Marnie chased each other up and down the grassy hills and around the lily ponds. They would also try to catch polliwogs. In the winter, they skated on the frozen ponds and raced down snow-covered banks. But for Ted, the best part of the park was always the zoo.

When Ted got home from his visits to the zoo, he would try to draw pictures of the monkeys and lions and wolves he had seen. Ted's mother, Henrietta Seuss Geisel, encouraged him. Sometimes she would even let him draw on the attic walls. But she usually gave him wallpaper scraps to use.

Ted's creatures did not look at all like the animals at the zoo. One of his beasts, a WYNNMPH, had ears three yards long. Ted's mother loved it.

When Ted was almost five, his eighteen-month-old sister, Henrietta, caught pneumonia. She coughed and coughed. There was no medicine to save her, and she died. Ted and Marnie missed her badly. Now it was just the two of them.

Their parents worked hard to make them feel happy and loved. Each summer, they took the children to a beach cottage near Clinton, Connecticut. They spent hours together, digging for clams or frolicking in the sand. Ted's father loved to fish. Sometimes he let Ted and Marnie pull in his catch. They often had to remind him to come in before the tide got too high. Then he would carry Ted and Marnie, one under each strong arm, through the rising tide back to shore.

Back in Springfield, the Forest Park Library, which was three blocks from their home, was a favorite place for family outings. Ted would choose stacks of books for his parents to read to him.

By the time he was six years old, Ted was reading stories for himself, some of them by Charles Dickens and Robert Louis Stevenson. One of Ted's best-loved books was *The Hole Book*. In it, a boy plays with a gun, and it goes off. The bullet flies through the house and pierces a water boiler, causing rooms to fill with water. The bullet keeps going, putting holes in everything in its way. Finally, it travels to the kitchen, where it hits a cake that is so hard that it stops the bullet.

Ted loved this book, and he pored over it until he knew it by heart.

No one knows if Ted's father or mother ever shot a hole through a cake, but they were both exceptionally skilled at rifle shooting. They were so good, in fact, that they took home medals and trophies from international competitions. At one time, Ted's father held the world's record for shooting at 200 yards. He practiced every morning for half an hour. To young Ted, target shooting seemed silly. But his father's determination taught him to "reach for excellence." Ted said he learned that "if you don't, you end up with schlock."

"Schlock" was a word Ted picked up from his parents and German grandparents. Both the Seuss and Geisel families had come to America from Germany. Ted and Marnie learned to speak German at an early age to understand what the grown-ups were saying.

Ted and Marnie saw much of Grandfather and Grandmother Geisel because they lived only a few blocks away. Ted's father worked in the brewery that Grandfather Geisel had started. The name of the brewery was Kalmbach and Geisel, but people jokingly called it "Come back and guzzle."

Ted was used to this kind of wordplay. Not only did he give strange names to his animals, he also put humorous words into their mouths.

When Ted was twelve, he entered an advertising contest sponsored by the local newspaper, *The Springfield Union.* Ted drew an ad for fishing tackle that showed a man reeling in a very big fish, and his cartoon won a prize. "That," Ted said, "was my first big bang!"

A tall, shy youngster, Ted had an easy smile and a twinkle in his eyes. He did well in his classes, and his friends liked his funny stories and cartoons. So he kept drawing.

In 1917, the United States started sending soldiers to Europe to fight in World War I. Everyone got involved in helping the soldiers. Marnie knitted stockings, while Ted sold thrift stamps and Liberty Bonds to raise money. Ted collected so much money (thanks mostly to Grandfather Geisel) that he placed second in a Boy Scout sales contest. He was chosen to receive a medal from the former president of the United States, Theodore Roosevelt.

On a bright Saturday morning, thirteen-year-old Ted and nine other boys sat in front of the city hall platform with its red, white, and blue ribbons, while Roosevelt finished his speech.

At last, it was time. The boys paraded onto the stage, and Theodore Roosevelt slowly proceeded down the line, shaking the boys' hands and then presenting them with medals. As he approached Ted, he stopped. He called the scoutmaster over and murmured something to him. The scoutmaster mumbled something back. Then the former president looked down at Ted and asked, "What are you doing here?"

Ted opened his mouth, but nothing came out. The next thing Ted knew, he was being guided—not too gently—off the stage. Someone had made a mistake. There were ten Boy Scouts and only nine medals. It was Ted's bad luck to be last in line. He was ashamed and embarrassed.

This incident did not help Ted's confidence. Yet he found ways to overcome his shyness. Awkward at sports, Ted chose to act in the school theater and to play tenor banjo in a jazz band. What he liked most of all, however, was making his friends laugh by writing or drawing something funny.

Red Smith, Ted's English teacher at Central High, helped Ted turn his ideas into stories, poems, jokes, and news articles. Ted's writing got better and better. Soon he was editing the school newspaper, the *Central Recorder*.

Though Ted's friends were impressed with his drawings, his art teacher was not. Once, in class, Ted turned his painting upside down to look at it.

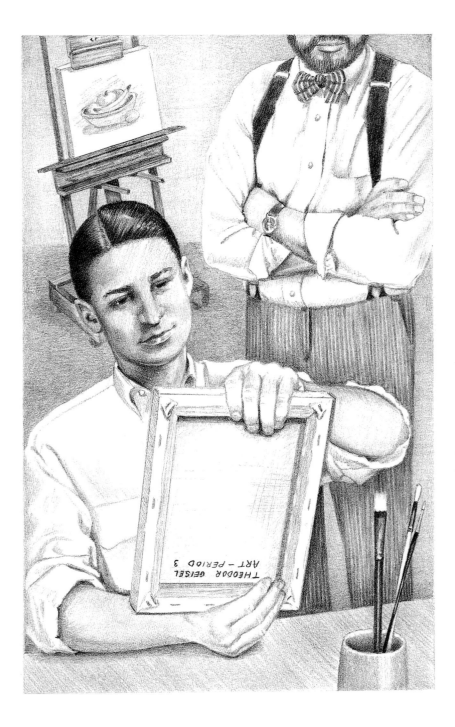

He wasn't exactly sure why he did it, but he found out later this is how an artist can check a painting's balance. If the painting is balanced, it will look good upside down or right side up.

His art teacher, however, thought Ted was fooling around and claimed that real artists never turned their paintings upside down. "That teacher wanted me to draw the world as it is," Ted said, "and I wanted to draw things as I saw them."

The teacher went so far as to advise Ted to try a career other than art. But Ted was stubborn. He resolved then and there to be an artist someday.

While Ted was in high school, his grandfather Geisel was preparing to retire from the brewery, and Ted's father was getting ready to take his place. However, there was one problem. On January 16, 1920, laws went into effect that made it illegal to make, sell, or drink alcohol of any kind.

Not surprisingly, the brewery went out of business and Ted's father was out of a job. Fortunately, he still had his volunteer position as chairman of the parks commission. So when the park superintendent retired, the city hired Ted R. Geisel.

Ted's father was thrilled with his new position. He put people to work building tennis courts, golf courses, trout streams, and bowling greens. Ted liked his father's new job too—since he now *ran* the zoo.

As graduation approached, he had to think about what to do next. Since his favorite teacher, Red Smith, had gotten his degree at Dartmouth College, Ted decided to go there.

In the fall of 1921, seventeen-year-old Ted moved on beyond Fairfield Street. He headed north a hundred and thirty miles along the Connecticut River to Hanover, New Hampshire, to begin life as a college freshman.

At Dartmouth, Ted found another English teacher who encouraged him to write. Professor Ben Pressey invited all his creative-writing students to his home and served them cocoa as they read their work aloud. Ted boasted to the class that he could write on any subject. To prove it, he composed a book review on the timetables for the Boston & Maine Railroad. "Nobody in the class thought it was funny," Ted admitted, "except Ben and me."

By the end of Ted's junior year at Dartmouth, he was editing the school's humor magazine, *Jack O'Lantern*. One of his cartoons showed two chimney sweeps on top of a chimney. The first said, "Should I go down first?" The other replied, "Soot yourself." This showed the wordplay Ted's classmates had learned to expect. Ted also wrote news for the college paper, the *Daily Dartmouth*.

Besides his work on the magazine and paper, Ted played mandolin in the orchestra, managed the soccer team, and argued about political issues for the debate team. But writing was still Ted's favorite "sport." He said, "It was a lot less dangerous than doing somersaults off the ski jump."

Ted and his college fraternity brothers liked making their own good times too. Because Ted socialized more than he studied, his friends named him the one "Least Likely to Succeed."

At one point, college officials decided Ted was having a little too much fun. It was the spring of 1925. Ted was finishing his senior year. The night before Easter, he invited ten people over for a party. The noise woke Ted's landlord, Pa Randall, who phoned the police chief. Ted was sent to Craven Laycock, dean of the college.

As punishment, Dean Laycock told Ted to resign as editor of the *Jack O'Lantern*. Ted, however, found a way around this. He kept editing, writing, and drawing cartoons as he always had. He just made up a new name for himself—Ted Seuss, or simply, Seuss.

2

On Beyond Dartmouth

Within months, Ted was going to graduate with a liberal arts degree. Then he'd have to get a job. He knew he could write and he could draw, but he wasn't sure he could make a living doing either one. Perhaps, though, he could work as a college professor. But to do this, he would have to obtain another degree.

Ted decided he should study in England, and he applied for the Campbell Fellowship in English Literature at Oxford University. He was so sure of himself that he wrote to his father and told him he was going to win it.

When his father got the letter, he ran across the street and told the good news to a neighbor, Maurice Sherman. Maurice was the editor of the *Springfield Union*. Sure enough, the front-page story the next day was "Geisel Wins Fellowship to Go to Oxford," complete with a picture of Ted.

As it turned out, though, Ted didn't receive the

award. His father was embarrassed. What could he do?

He sent Ted to Oxford and paid for it himself.

In the fall of 1925, Ted packed his bags and traveled across the ocean to Lincoln College, Oxford. He sat in class and tried to take notes on Shakespeare. But winged horses and flying cows kept appearing in the margins of his notebook.

One time in class, a petite, dark-haired American student named Helen Palmer looked over at Ted's drawings and said, "I think that's a very good flying cow." She suggested that Ted quit studying literature and work at drawing instead.

Ted liked Helen's idea. (He liked Helen too.) While Helen was riding on the back of his motorcycle one day, Ted asked her to marry him.

She said yes, and Ted got so excited he ran off the road and into a ditch. Luckily, neither of them was injured.

Luckily, too, Ted was not caught riding his motorcycle. Oxford students were forbidden to own them. But, once again, Ted found a way around the rules. He tied two dead ducks to his handlebars. This made it look like the motorcycle belonged to someone else who sold poultry for a living.

Despite Helen's encouragement, Ted did not believe he could get a job as an artist. He thought it would be more practical for him to become an English teacher so he and Helen could afford to get married. To finish his degree, he had to do a research project. He was assigned the task of finding out whether or not the writer Jonathan Swift had written anything between the ages of sixteen and seventeen. Ted didn't think anyone would care if Swift had or not. It made Ted wonder if he really wanted to be a college teacher.

In June 1926, Ted's family came to visit him. Together, they traveled throughout Great Britain, France, Switzerland, and Germany (where they visited distant relatives). That summer, Ted decided not to go back to Oxford. Helen stayed in England to finish her degree, while Ted went to Paris to study with an Oxford writing professor at the Sorbonne.

Ted later joked that he went to classes for a month before he realized he didn't understand a word of French. He left Paris and took a cattle boat to Corsica, a French island in the Mediterranean Sea. There he spent a month painting pictures of donkeys.

This did not convince him he could earn money as an artist. Perhaps he would try writing again. So he sat down to create a great novel. This did not go as he had planned either. Afterward, Ted claimed that he had written entire chapters of the book in Italian. "I don't even speak Italian," he said. "I couldn't understand a word of it." As strange as this may seem, Ted swore it was true. He eventually boiled the whole book down to a two-line cartoon.

Turning the Corner
on Mulberry Street

Returning from Europe in the spring of 1927, twenty-three-year-old Ted went back to his parents' home on Fairfield Street. He had no money, no job, and no career. The one thing Ted *knew* he knew how to do was draw cartoons. He sent hundreds of his crazy animals to one magazine after another. But nobody wanted eggnog-drinking turtles or his other wild-looking creatures.

After several weeks of rejection slips, the *Saturday Evening Post* bought one of Ted's cartoons for twenty-five dollars. Ted was thrilled. Helen was already working as a teacher in New Jersey, and if he could earn some money too, they could get married.

It was time, Ted thought, to be on his own. He hopped a train for New York City. There he rented a tiny apartment in Greenwich Village with an artist, John C. Rose. It was a cheap, dismal place over a nightclub called the Pirate's Den. Every night, rats tried to come into their rooms to escape the cold. Ted and John would stand on chairs and chase them out with long-handled canes and brooms.

It took several months, but Ted finally sold a turtle cartoon to a magazine called *Judge*. What was more, they offered him a job as a staff writer and artist. Ted jumped at the chance. After all, they would pay him seventy-five dollars a week. Ted thought he had landed on top of the world.

Ted and Helen were married in Westfield, New Jersey, on November 29, 1927. Because they did not have much money, they rented an apartment across from a stable in the Hell's Kitchen area of New York City. Ted remembered, "Horses frequently died in the stable, and they'd drag them out and leave them in the street, where they'd be picked up by sanitation two or three days later."

A little while after the couple was settled, *Judge* started having money problems. They lowered Ted's salary to fifty dollars a week. Often they did not even pay him this. Instead of a paycheck,

Ted would receive products the magazine had been given by its advertisers. Once, Ted's pay was 100 cartons of Barbasol shaving cream. Another time, he took home 1,872 Little Gem nail clippers. Despite the ups and downs, Ted felt fortunate. He was making a living doing something he loved: drawing. Other magazines were buying his work too: *Life*, *Redbook*, *Vanity Fair*. What was better, these journals paid him in money—not shaving cream or nail clippers.

Ted started doing a regular cartoon feature for *Judge* called "Boids and Beasties." The pieces were about animals—part truth, mostly fiction. He signed them "Dr. Theophrastus Seuss" to make them seem more professional. (He wanted to save his real name for the great novel he still hoped to write someday.) Soon he was signing Dr. Seuss on all his work. Ted bragged that he saved his father thousands of dollars by becoming a doctor without going to medical school.

One cartoon for *Judge* changed Ted's life. It pictured a knight lying on his bed, obviously exhausted. A dragon pokes his head in the knight's face, and the knight says, "Darn it all, another dragon! And just after I'd sprayed the whole castle with Flit." (Flit was a popular insect repellent.)

The cartoon attracted the attention of Mrs. Lincoln Cleaves, the wife of an advertising executive for Flit. After two weeks of pestering from his wife, Mr. Cleaves gave Ted a call.

Soon Ted was producing ads promoting Flit. He drew outlandish insects and created a phrase that caught on in households across America: "Quick, Henry, the Flit!"

At twenty-seven years old, Ted was earning $12,000 a year. That was a lot of money for a young couple in 1931—especially since the nation was struggling through a time of depression, in which many people had lost their jobs and businesses. Yet Ted and Helen now found they could afford one of New York's fancy Park Avenue apartments. They moved north to 79th Street and West End Avenue.

Ted described the advantages of the location by saying, "There were many fewer dead horses."

However, there was one thing wrong with the apartment. The Geisel's phone number differed by one digit from that of the local fish market. Each time someone called to order fish, Ted would draw a fish on cardboard and have it delivered. He never told the customers they had a wrong number.

Neither Ted nor Helen liked to cook—fish, or

anything else. Once when Ted's mother came to visit, she opened the refrigerator and could hardly believe her eyes. The only thing in it was a cookbook she had given them for a wedding present. Ted explained that since he was an artist, he had to visit restaurants to observe people.

Not long after they had moved, Ted's mother began having headaches and falling asleep while playing bridge with her friends. In 1931, after much persuading, Ted's father convinced her to see a prominent brain surgeon. The doctor operated and found she had a brain tumor. There was nothing he could do. She died soon after the operation.

Despite his grief, Ted continued to do well in his job. The only problem was that he wasn't busy enough. Since bug spray is primarily a spring and summer product, Ted had about seven months to do nothing. He and Helen traveled, but that wasn't enough. "I was successful but frustrated," he said.

Ted didn't sit and wait for something to happen. He checked his contract and found that it didn't prevent him from writing children's books. In 1932, he wrote and illustrated an ABC book. It contained his usual array of way-out animals—

including a long-necked whizzleworp.

No publisher would buy it.

Ted, though, didn't give up. In the summer of 1936, he and Helen were returning from a holiday in Europe aboard the ship the *M. S. Kungsholm.* To keep his mind off a storm that battered the vessel, Ted sat in the bar and scratched out phrases on the ship's stationery. The rhythm of the engines attracted him, and he tried to conjure up words to match the beat.

After several tries, he found ones he liked: "And to think that I saw it on Mulberry Street." (Mulberry Street is a street in Springfield, where his father had attended school.) These ten words formed the beginning of Ted's first children's story. It is a tale of a boy's fanciful journey home from school.

Writing it proved easier than selling it. Twenty-seven publishers rejected the story.

Ted was discouraged. One day as he was walking down a New York City street, he met a college friend, Marshall (Mike) McClintock. Mike had just become an editor of books for children at Vanguard Press. He needed manuscripts to publish, and Ted needed a publisher. So they made a deal.

And to Think That I Saw It on Mulberry Street

came out in 1937. It sold for one dollar, which was expensive at that time. Even so, the book quickly sold more than 10,000 copies. Mike called to say, "Congratulations! You *are* an author!" Noted children's author Beatrix Potter called it "the cleverest book I have met with for many years."

Ted had discovered he loved writing for children, and they seemed to love what he wrote. They could be strong critics, however. Shortly after *Mulberry Street* was published, Ted presented a program onstage at Higbee's Department Store in Cleveland. Three hundred third graders shuffled in and sat down. Up front, Ted drew frantically for them. No response. Finally he asked his audience, "Don't you like my drawing?"

"No," they said, "Gus can draw better." So Ted called Gus up onto the stage. Sure enough, Gus *could* draw better.

Nevertheless, inspired by the reviews he received for *Mulberry Street*, Ted began looking for a subject for another children's book. One morning, he was on a commuter train. "There was a fellow sitting ahead of me," said Ted, "who I didn't like. He had a real ridiculous Wall Street broker's hat on—very stuffy. And I just began playing around with the idea of what his reaction would be if I took his hat off and threw it out the window. And I said [to myself], 'He'd probably just grow another one and ignore me.'"

This funny thought grew into *The 500 Hats of Bartholomew Cubbins*, which Vanguard Press published in 1938. Ted dedicated the book to his imaginary child, Chrysanthemum-Pearl, "aged 89 months, going on 90." According to Ted, Chrysanthemum was a clever child who liked to knit red long underwear for her Uncle Terwilliger and make oyster stew with chocolate frosting. When Ted's fans heard about the youngster, they sent her gifts.

People often asked Ted why he and Helen did not have children. Ted would reply, "You have 'em, I'll amuse 'em." However, there was one child whom they both loved—Peggy, the only child of Ted's sister Marnie and her husband.

The Geisels would look forward to seeing her whenever they visited Springfield, and when Peggy was eleven, they invited her to New York City to go with them to the 1939 World's Fair.

For one wonderful week, the three went to the fair every day. It was a child's dream come true.

On his way to becoming a full-time children's author, Ted quit his job writing ads for Flit. In 1939, Ted sold a second story about Bartholomew.

It was called *The King's Stilts*, and this time he sold it to Random House Publishers. In 1940, *Horton Hatches the Egg* was greeted by eager fans. Ted also published a picture book for adults, *The Seven Lady Godivas*. It was rejected by most everyone. It was just a little too silly for grown-ups to take it seriously.

At the same time, Helen was also making a name for herself in children's books. In 1944, two of her works were published: *Three Caballeros* and *Walt Disney's Surprise Package*.

While Ted and Helen's lives were blossoming, Marnie's was closing in on her. She suffered from agoraphobia—a fear of seeing strangers and being in public places. She withdrew from friends and family, and her health began to fail. In September 1945, Marnie died at the age of forty-three.

Not long afterward, her daughter Peggy went off to college, but she kept in contact with Ted and Helen. She knew she could always turn to them when she needed them. Their house became her second home.

4

Out in Left Field

During the 1940s, World War II blazed over Europe, changing the lives of many people. Ted decided to use his talents to help the war effort. He and Helen moved to Hollywood. Ted was made a captain and was assigned to work with movie director Frank Capra to develop instructional films for soldiers. Capra showed Ted how to edit a script and throw out parts that did not move the story along. Ted saw how this kind of editing would help his children's books.

Ted received the Legion of Merit Award for his film in the *Why We Fight* movie series and an Academy Award for *Hitler Lives*. This movie was named best short documentary of 1946. A year later, Ted won another Academy Award for a documentary film on Japan.

After the war, Ted and Helen decided to stay on in California. The Geisels found an observation tower on six and a half acres of land north of San Diego in a town called La Jolla. A real-estate salesman had built the tower on Mount Soledad, the highest spot in the area, to show his customers the view. It hadn't been used for years. The closets were full of empty beer cans, and the walls were thick with painted initials surrounded by hearts.

The Geisels bought the tower in 1948 and added pink stucco rooms around it. They cleaned out the beer cans but left some hearts.

Now Ted *was* on top of the world. At least, that was how he felt. He made the upper tower space into his workroom. Using a drafting table for a desk, he propped his typewriter along the top edge. As he sat at this table, he could gaze over his left shoulder at the Pacific Ocean. Up the coast lay San Juan Capistrano. To the south was Mexico. On a clear day, he could see San Clemente Island, about seventy-five miles out at sea.

Ted forced himself to stay in his workroom eight hours a day, every day of the week. The cork-lined walls of the room were soon hidden under layers of drawings. When Ted started working on a book, he would make his first drawings on tissue or tracing paper. He would then pen in the pictures and words for one page, and then move on to the next.

Normally, at the end of the day, the studio floor and wastebasket were piled high with sheets of discarded paper. Ted nicknamed the heaps the "bone pile." Once he had drawn and written each page of his book over and over, he would make his final drawings on heavy paper, using felt-tip pens.

Still, Ted sometimes didn't have an idea in the world. He might lie the whole day long on the floor, staring at the ceiling, "puzzling my puzzler," as he would say. If he was stuck in midthought or midbook, he would pace the floor. If that didn't help, he would run down the stairs to the lower tower room. (Eventually he moved his studio there.) He would throw himself down on the day bed and thrash around like a wild man or grab the brown stuffed dog from his childhood and toss it up and down.

Finally, if no inspiration struck him, he would yank out a thinking cap from his hat collection. It might be an old war helmet or the Duke of Luxembourg's top hat (or so he said). Whatever it was, a hat usually did the trick.

Ted tried to work *only* eight hours a day. But if ideas started flowing, he would work late into the night and sometimes until morning. People often asked Ted where he found his ideas. Ted liked to respond that he found them out in left field. If he couldn't find them there, he would travel to an Arizona desert, where he would pick the brain of a retired thunderbird. Ted said he had no idea where the thunderbird got his ideas.

One time Ted told an audience that he collected all his ideas in Switzerland, in a tiny town called Zybilknov. "I go there every year on the fourth of August to have my cuckoo clock fixed," he explained. "While I am waiting for my clock, I walk the streets of the village and talk to some of its strange inhabitants. That is where I get the ideas for the characters in my books."

In truth, his ideas often sprang from chance encounters. During the war, Ted had traveled to France for a movie project. He and the other soldiers had slogged through deep mud. Rain had been coming down for weeks. One soldier stopped Ted and asked, "Why is it always rain? Can't anything else come down?" Later, in his tower, Ted wondered if maybe some green stuff called oobleck could come down. *Bartholomew and the Oobleck* was published by Random House in 1949. It won a Caldecott Honor Book Award from the American Library Association in 1950.

Thidwick the Big-Hearted Moose began with a

doodle Ted made while talking on the phone to his friend Joe Warwick. Ted named the doodled moose "Warwick" in honor of Joe. But eventually the moose started to look more like a Thidwick, and that's how he stayed.

While ideas were springing into Ted's mind from all directions, Helen was busy writing more children's books too. In the late 1940s, three of her books were published by Simon & Schuster. Besides writing, Helen assisted Ted in answering the many fan letters now delivered for Dr. Seuss. She signed them "Mrs. Dr. Seuss." Peggy also helped out with secretarial chores when she stayed with them. Finally, Ted hired a part-time secretary to answer all the phone calls and handle the mail.

The Geisels often worked together on projects. Ted did not like criticism, but he would take it from Helen—even ask for it—because he respected her opinions. Ted called her his best critic. She would help him stick to his story line. He said "Helen edits all my books—and handles the business affairs. She has to—if I had to cope with accounts, we'd be in desperate trouble."

Ted didn't carry money, and he could not balance a checkbook. Sometimes he and Helen would go out to dinner with friends, and Ted would offer to pick up the check. Then he'd realize he didn't have a cent on him.

Though Ted was still shy, he could take a stand in public when he believed something needed to be done. He served as a trustee of the San Diego Fine Arts Gallery and became involved in the La Jolla Town Council. When more and more billboards began popping up and ruining the local scenery, Ted wrote and illustrated a brochure for a campaign to ban offensive and unnecessary signs.

In 1951, Ted had a chance to combine writing children's stories with filmmaking. He wrote the script for an animated cartoon: *Gerald McBoing Boing*. It was the story of a boy who doesn't speak words but "goes Boing boing instead." Ted chose not to do the illustrations because he did not think he drew people very well. The film earned Ted his third Academy Award.

Lured back into moviemaking, Ted thought he would try a children's film that featured real children. It was entitled *The 5,000 Fingers of Dr. T.* Ted called it "the worst experience of my life."

Everything seemed to go wrong. The lowest point came when someone paid the five hundred child actors directly instead of giving the money to their parents or agents. The kids ran to the lunchroom and stuffed themselves with hot dogs. When they returned to the set, one child threw up, and the rest followed suit. Ted had had enough.

During the early 1950s, Ted had more significant struggles to face. Helen lost the use of her mouth, hands, arms, and legs. It was a rare form of paralysis, and she nearly died. Ted was devastated. He could not imagine life without her.

When Helen went to a hospital in Santa Monica to learn to walk and talk again, Ted rented an apartment nearby so he could be with her as much as possible. After several months, Helen regained enough use of her muscles to return to La Jolla. For the rest of her life, however, Helen suffered from a lingering tightness in her legs and feet.

By the spring of 1956, Helen was well enough to accompany Ted to Dartmouth College where he received an honorary doctorate degree. Now Ted *was* Dr. Seuss. The college president praised him: "As author and artist, you single-handedly have stood as Saint George between a generation of parents and the demon dragon of exhausted children on a rainy day." It was one of the proudest moments of Ted's life.

The next year held more life-changing events for the Geisels. It was the year of the Grinch.

Ted had been thinking about the meaning of Christmas for about twelve years. He hated the fact that most people ran around buying things that other people didn't really want or need. He wished everyone would think more about love than about gifts. So when Random House gave him a deadline for a Christmas book, Ted sat down and wrote it in one week.

That was, until he came to the last page. Ted lamented, "I worked on the ending for two and a half months. I tried hundreds of endings before I found just the right one."

When someone asked him how he came up with the name Grinch, he answered, "It was simple. I just drew him and looked at him, and it was obvious to me who he was."

The Grinch became one of Ted's favorite characters. He often joked that he was part Grinch himself. Maybe so, maybe not. But the license plate on Ted's steel-gray Cadillac Seville bore the name GRINCH.

In the Beginning
Was the Cat

In addition to the Grinch, 1957 was the year of the Cat. Ted brought forth *The Cat in the Hat*, and a new era in children's books was born.

The book came into being—as many great things do—quite by accident. Ted read an article in *Life* magazine criticizing the "Dick and Jane" books that were used to teach children to read. John Hersey, the author of the article, suggested that Dr. Seuss could create better beginner readers for children. John Hersey may have meant it as a joke, but Ted took the challenge seriously.

Ted talked to Random House about it, and he was handed a list of 223 easy-to-read words and told to go to work. Ted thought it would be simple. Surely he could make a book out of those words in a week. In fact, it took nine months of thrashing around and throwing the manuscript across the room to create *The Cat in the Hat*. It happened then only because "cat" and "hat" were the first two words on the list that rhymed.

The book did not sell well to schools, but when Random House took it to bookstores, the cat in the tall striped hat bounded off the shelves.

A sign soon appeared on Ted's house: "Beware of the Cat." Strangely enough, though the Geisels had a steady string of pet cats, Ted never really liked cats; Helen did. But scattered around their home were several of his drawings of cats—a cat in a gondola was called "O Sole Meow." Another sketch was entitled "A Cat in a Cradle Making a Cat's Cradle." Ted said that he really liked dogs better, but he never learned to draw dogs.

Because of the great success of *The Cat in the Hat*, Random House developed a division called Beginner Books, which specialized in fun-filled first readers for kids. They put Ted in charge of it. Helen became the vice president, and the Cat in the Hat appeared on the covers of all the books.

Both Ted and Helen wrote and edited books in the series. Some of Ted's best-known titles were *Hop on Pop, Fox in Socks*, and *One Fish, Two Fish, Red Fish, Blue Fish*. With a few Beginner Books, Ted gave his name a new twist. Whenever he wrote a story for which he hired someone else to draw the pictures, he called himself Theo LeSieg—Geisel spelled backward.

One of Ted's most famous books, *Green Eggs and Ham*, came about because of another challenge. Editor Bennett Cerf bet Ted fifty dollars he couldn't write a book using *only* fifty simple words. Ted proved to him and the world he could. Yet sometimes he complained about having taken that bet. Almost every time he was invited to a banquet, the menu included green eggs and ham.

Although they were now working more closely with Random House, Ted and Helen stayed in La Jolla. When Ted finished a manuscript, he would fly to New York and read it aloud to the other editors at Random House. But the night before he would leave, he often could not sleep. So he would lay out the pages on the floor and call his neighbor, Bert Hupp. Bert was in his seventies and was the former chairman of the board of the Sunshine Biscuit Company. Ted trusted Bert's judgment because Bert would tell Ted if anything didn't look right. Most of the time, Bert said the book looked great. Then Ted could go back to bed.

Ted believed it was essential that his books be funny. Once after he presented a book to

Random House, he went back to his hotel and spent a week rewriting three pages because they were not funny enough.

Humor, he said, was an important way of keeping the right outlook on the world. If you could look at a situation when it was out of whack, then you could see how it could be "in whack." He said, "I prefer to look at things through the wrong end of the telescope."

Some of Ted's characters seemed extremely "whacky," but he claimed they were all based on real animals. "I have a special dictionary of them," he would explain, "and I just look up the spellings." Helen would laugh and add, "His mind has never grown up."

Helen was not alone in observing this. When Ted decided to quit smoking, he bought himself a corn-cob pipe, and in the bowl of the pipe, he planted radish seeds. Then he boarded a bus, holding the unlit pipe in his mouth.

After a few minutes, he reached into his pocket, pulled out an eyedropper, and watered the contents of the pipe.

"What are you doing?" a woman asked.

"I'm watering the radishes," Ted replied, with a smile in his eyes.

Although Ted did some things that did not seem logical, there was always a logic to what Ted's characters said and did. If, for example, he drew a creature with two heads, he made sure it had two hats and two toothbrushes.

Ted explained, "My animals look the way they do because I can't draw." He called his method "exaggerated mistakes." Once Ted was supposed to draw a goat for an advertising billboard. The ad executive thought the goat resembled a duck. So Ted drew him a duck. The client thought it was a terrific goat.

Whether he was writing or drawing, Ted said that the creative process consisted of only two things: time and sweat. He believed that writing a children's book was just as much work as writing an adult novel. "Children are a tough audience," Ted said. "You can fool an adult audience with persiflage or purple prose, but a kid can tell if you're faking immediately." Ted was most pleased when he could make a child laugh. One nine-year-old fan wrote of a Dr. Seuss book: "It's the funniest book I ever read in nine years."

Ted's fan letters—which now averaged between 1,500 and 2,000 a week—often mentioned how much the readers liked his rhymes. By the time Ted was in his sixties, he had written in verse so long he would dream in rhyme. He even had trouble writing a short letter without the words rhyming.

When Ted was sixty-three, he lost his business partner, vice president, chief critic, and the woman he loved: Helen Palmer Geisel. On October 23, 1967, Helen died at home.

There was no funeral. Instead, the La Jolla Museum of Art held a ceremony naming their new library the Helen Palmer Geisel Library.

The next year for Ted was filled with more sorrow. Ted's father died at the age of eighty-nine, and his son felt this loss deeply.

Fortunately, however, Ted found someone to share both sadness and celebration. Audrey Stone Dimond had been a friend to both Ted and Helen for several years, and now she became Ted's wife. She was the mother of two teenage daughters, Leagrey and Lark. The girls attended boarding schools most of the year, but Ted liked to tease and entertain them when they were home.

Despite the great success of Dr. Seuss, Ted and Audrey lived a fairly simple lifestyle. They had one car, a swimming pool, and a part-time maid. They hired a gardener, but even so, Ted enjoyed spending spare moments tending their rock garden.

When Ted was not writing, drawing, or rock gardening, he was usually reading. He read four or five books a week. He preferred paperbacks—mostly history, biographies, and detective stories. Ted also read at least one newspaper a day. He once tried to subscribe to two papers, but Cluny, his Irish setter, had other ideas. Cluny was used to retrieving one morning paper, and when Ted ordered a second, Cluny promptly buried it.

As Ted grew older, he lost none of his love for mischief. When Ted and Audrey invited a retired navy officer to join them and some friends for dinner, the very proper gentleman asked how he should dress. Ted told him to wear formal clothes. The night of the party, the man appeared in his navy uniform, complete with a stiff white shirt. After dinner, he fell asleep in a chair.

Ted couldn't help himself. He took out his pens and drew Dr. Seuss characters all over the front of his friend's starched white shirt.

6

Climbing Mount Everest

As Ted entered his late sixties, he became more willing to express his political concerns openly in his books. *The Lorax* grew out of Ted's anger at the damage that was being done to the earth, water, and air. He had an idea of what he wanted to write, but he was having trouble getting the story the way he wanted it. So he left the manuscript at home, and he and Audrey flew to Africa. As Ted sat on the edge of a swimming pool in Kenya, he spotted a herd of elephants coming over the hill. The scene triggered something in his mind. He found a pad of paper and wrote the whole book that afternoon.

The Lorax was published in 1971, and it has been considered a classic book about caring for the environment ever since. That same year, Ted also made his mark in television. He received two Peabody Awards for his TV specials, *How the Grinch Stole Christmas* and *Horton Hears a Who.*

Though Dr. Seuss and his books seemed ageless, Ted was beginning to feel his age and experience the health problems that went with it. He was advised to cut back on ham and eggs—even green eggs—and to be careful of other things he ate. In 1978 and 1980, he underwent cataract surgeries on his eyes. After each operation, his eyes had to adjust and relearn how to see shades of color. Hard as it was on him, Ted joked, "Now they claim I'll be as good as Picasso."

By the time Ted reached the age of seventy-five, there were forty-two Dr. Seuss books in print. Eighty million copies had been sold, and the books had been translated into more than twenty languages, including Maori, Japanese, and Dutch. Random House declared May 1979 Dr. Seuss Month.

Although Ted had already accomplished so much, he still put in eight hours a day writing and drawing. Why? Because he loved it. From the windows of his studio he could see his retired friends sailing on the Pacific. But retirement was not for him.

On his eightieth birthday, March 2, 1984, Random House threw a party for him at the New York Public Library. At the celebration, a new Dr. Seuss title was introduced: *The Butter Battle Book*. Ted wrote it to make people think about the dangers of nuclear weapons. It held the honor of being the only children's book to appear for six months on the *New York Times* best-seller list for *adults*.

That year, Ted was also presented with his greatest honor. It was a special award from the Pulitzer Prize Committee for his lifetime of contributions to children's literature. Ted was completely surprised when he received the call saying he had won. He had just been having a lot of trouble with a drawing and was feeling like a failure.

Persevering through a heart attack and several bouts with throat cancer, Ted continued to work. At the age of eighty-two, Ted told a reporter, "Age has no effect on me. I surf as much as I always have! I climb Mount Everest as much as I always have!" Certainly, Ted wrote and drew as much as he always had. In fact, in 1986, his book *You're Only Old Once*, subtitled *A Book for Obsolete Children*, was published.

"Obsolete children" was Ted's name for adults. This book took shape during some of Ted's many long waits in the doctor's offices. To pass the time, he had started sketching what he saw, and later he put words to the drawings.

You're Only Old Once also made the *New York Times* adult best-seller list. In a New York City bookstore, thirteen hundred people stood in line to get Ted's autograph on the book. Ted joked, "Thank God my name isn't Henry Wadsworth Longfellow."

Ted's next book was for both grown-ups and kids. *Oh, the Places You'll Go* encouraged readers to try new things, to take chances, to go places.

Ted's experiments in life had led him to children's books, and his work in books and art had made him happy. So he generously supported libraries as well as art museums. Ted formed the Dr. Seuss Foundation to donate money to scholarships, to various charities, and, of course, to zoos.

Where kids were involved, Ted was always ready to give of his time and his money. He helped raise money for San Diego Youth and Community Services by donating autographed copies of his books for a fund-raising auction. In exchange for some of Ted's books, the rock group Aerosmith donated a signed guitar that brought in $3,500.

Another time, La Jolla High School needed money to send two students to a Science Olympiad. For their event, called The Scrambler, the students designed a vehicle that could propel an egg at high speed for ten meters. At the end was a solid wall. A faulty design would result in a scrambled egg. Ted sent a check with a note that read, "Scrambling has always been my favorite Olympic sport."

Ted was always generous with Dartmouth College too. He gave the school first editions of all his books and the original manuscript for *The 500 Hats of Bartholomew Cubbins*. Dartmouth students will also remember Ted whenever they attend a humanities program sponsored by the Geisel Professorship fund.

Ted kept working into his late eighties. Not long before he died, a friend, Neil Morgan, asked him if he had any words of wisdom to leave to the world. Ted thought a minute and then said, "Whenever things go a bit sour in a job I'm doing, I always tell myself: 'You can do better than this.' The best slogan I can think of to leave with the U.S.A. would be: 'We can do and we've got to do better than this.'"

Ted had put up a good battle against throat cancer. But on Tuesday, September 24, 1991, he lost the fight. Ted Seuss Geisel died at his home in La Jolla at the age of eighty-seven. Audrey, his wife, and Leagrey, his stepdaughter, were with him.

Notes of sympathy poured in from all over the country. First Lady Barbara Bush expressed her sorrow at the loss of one of her family's favorite authors. One first-grade girl said to a reporter that she would have liked to have told him "that we're going to miss him . . . that we love him . . . and we'll always remember him until the day he comes back alive."

Afterword

By the time Ted died, he had written and illustrated forty-eight books, which together had sold more than 200 million copies. He had spent the last year and a half of his life working on the animation for *Oh, the Places You'll Go.* It would have been the first full-length feature film based on one of his books. His last book, one of his favorites, was a collection of six previously published books called *Six By Seuss.*

Ted left behind a body of work that will endure for generations. Following Ted's wishes, Audrey donated over 4,000 pieces of his original artwork, manuscripts, and other memorabilia to the University of California at San Diego. The University of California at Los Angeles also has a large portion of Ted's work.

Random House, Ted's longtime publisher, honored his contribution to children's literature by establishing the Dr. Seuss Picture Book Award.

The award carries a $25,000 cash prize plus a publishing contract for a first-time author/illustrator.

In celebration of the joy that Ted brought to others, Balboa Park and the San Diego Zoo hosted a party on Sunday, November 17, 1991. They called it "Sunday in the Park with Seuss." Seventy-five thousand people ate green eggs and ham and crawled through a machine that put stars on their bellies.

Residents of Springfield, Massachusetts, plan to build a statue in memory of Ted near the city's library and museums. There is also talk of naming all or part of the Forest Park Zoo after Ted and of creating a Dr. Seuss trail in the neighborhood where Ted grew up.

Through his books, Ted transported readers to faraway lands, to the top of Horton's tree, and to the depths of McElligot's pool. With gentleness and humor, Ted guided both children and adults in thinking about the world from every possible viewpoint. Oh, the places we've gone, and will continue to go, thanks to Theodor Seuss Geisel.

Bibilography

Primary Sources

Interviews with: Steven L. Brezzo, director of San Diego Museum of Art; Tom Costello, president of Springfield Library and Museums; Kenneth Cramer, former Dartmouth College archivist; Don Freeman, free-lance reporter; Richard Garvey, editor of Springfield newspapers; Jeanne Jones, cookbook author and friend of Ted and Audrey Geisel; Guy McLain, head of library archives of Connecticut Valley Historical Museum; Peggy Owens, Ted's niece; Claudia Prescott, secretary to Ted and Audrey Geisel; Mardi Snow, public relations coordinator of the San Diego Museum of Art; Mary Stofflet, curator of the San Diego Museum of Art; and Lynn Whitehouse, librarian at La Jolla Public Library. *Thanks to all of you, who took the time to share knowledge and/or funny stories of a man we all loved and respected.*

Secondary Sources

Bandler, Michael J. "Seuss on the Loose." *Parents Magazine,* September 1987.

Bunzel, Peter. "Wacky World of Dr. Seuss." *Life*, 6 April 1959.

Cahn, Robert. "The Wonderful World of Dr. Seuss." *Saturday Evening Post*, 6 July 1957.

"Dr. Seuss." *Life*, July 1989.

Dr. Seuss from Then to Now: A Catalogue of the Retrospective Exhibition. Organized by the San Diego Museum of Art, San Diego, CA. New York: Random House, 1986.

Freeman, Don. "Dr. Seuss from Then to Now." *San Diego Magazine*, May 1986.

Gorney, Cynthia. "Dr. Seuss." *Washington Post*, 21 May 1979.

Harper, Hilliard. "The Private World of Dr. Seuss." *Los Angeles Times Magazine*, 25 May 1986.

Kahn, E. J. "Profiles: 'Children's Friend.'" *New Yorker*, 17 December 1960.

Katz, Lee Michael. "Most Kids Say Yooks Should Talk to Zooks." *USA Today*, 29 June 1984.

Kupferberg, Herbert. "A Seussian Celebration." *Parade Magazine*, 26 February 1984.

Lathem, Edward Connery. "The Beginnings of Dr. Seuss." *Dartmouth Alumni Magazine*, April 1976.

LeDradec, Pascale. "For Teachers, Kids, Dr. Seuss Lives On." *San Diego Tribune*, 26 September 1991.

Moore, Anne Caroll. "The Three Owls' Notebook." *The Horn Book Magazine*, January/February 1938.

Sheff, David. "Seuss on Wry." *Parenting Magazine*, February 1987.

Sullivan, Robert. "Oh, the Places He Went!" *Dartmouth Alumni Magazine*, Winter 1991.

Wilder, Rob. "Catching Up with Dr. Seuss." *Parents Magazine*, June 1979.